EXECUTIVE EDITORS
Mike Mifsud, Alan Doan, Jenny Doan,
Sarah Galbraith, David Mifsud

MANAGING EDITOR
Natalie Earnheart

CREATIVE DIRECTOR
Christine Ricks

PHOTOGRAPHY TEAM
Mike Brunner, Lauren Dorton, Jennifer Dowling,
Dustin Weant

PATTERN TEAM
Edie McGinnis, Denise Lane, Jessica Toye,
Tyler MacBeth

PROJECT DESIGN TEAM
Jenny Doan, Natalie Earnheart, Janet Yamamoto

EDITOR & COPYWRITERS
Jenny Doan, Natalie Earnheart, Katie Mifsud,
Camille Maddox, Nichole Spravzoff, Julie Barber,
David Litherland, Edie McGinnis

SEWIST TEAM
Jenny Doan, Natalie Earnheart, Janet Yamamoto,
Carol Henderson, Denise Lane, Janice Richardson,
Jamey Stone

QUILTING & BINDING DEPARTMENT
Ren Eide, Becky Bowen, Sandy Childs, Amy Turpin,
Nikki LaPiana, Debbie Allen, Victoria Swieger, Glenda
Rorabough, Bernice Kelly, Deloris Burnett, Darlene
Smith, Todd Harman, Debbie Elder, Jessica Paup, Jan
Meek, Kristin Cash, Lois Eckerts, Natalie Loucks, Holly
Clevenger, Willie Morgan, Linda Frump, Nora Clutter,
Lyndia Lovell, Rachael Joyce, Leta Eaton, Roxana
Hinkle, Jackie Jones, Salena Smiley, Francesca Fleming

LOCATION CREDIT
Mari's House Bed and Breakfast
200 East School Street
Hamilton, Mo. 64644

Morrell Ranch
21708 Nickle Ave
Gallatin, MO 64640

Sarah & Seth Galbraith home, Hamilton, MO

PRINTING COORDINATORS
Rob Stoebener, Seann Dwyer

PRINTING SERVICES
Walsworth Print Group
803 South Missouri
Marceline, MO 64658

CONTACT US
Missouri Star Quilt Company
114 N Davis
Hamilton, MO 64644
888-571-1122
info@missouriquiltco.com

BLOCK Idea Book™ Early Winter Volume 5 Issue 6
©2018. All Rights Reserved by Missouri Star Quilt
Company. Reproduction in whole or in part in any
language without written permission from Missouri
Star Quilt Company or BLOCK Idea Book is prohibited.
No one may copy, reprint, or distribute any of the
patterns or materials in this magazine for commercial
use without written permission of Missouri Star Quilt
Company. Anything you make using our patterns or
ideas is your business, do whatever you want with the
stuff you make, it's yours!

P9-DGK-637

content

2

Oops! Sometimes we make mistakes.
To find corrections to every issue of Block
go to: www.msqc.co/corrections

3

hello
from MSQC

Have you noticed a new feature on social media that reminds you of memories from previous months or years? It just popped up on my phone this week and reminded me of a beautiful vacation to a tropical place that I'd taken a couple years ago. The photos had been selected for me and there was even a bouncy soundtrack to accompany them. It was amazing! I hadn't thought of that trip for some time and it brightened up my morning. Back in the day, I would have had to pull down a photo album off of a dusty shelf to review memories of the past—not to mention the effort of putting that album together in the first place! Now photo albums come together like magic.

With memories more accessible than ever, I can't help but reminisce about the past year and look forward to what's coming next! I've always loved New Year's Eve. I anticipate the countdown eagerly with a noisemaker in hand. That moment is so full of possibility. When the new year begins, I can choose what I will do with it. The same is true for each day. As the poet Emily Dickinson once said, I like to "dwell in possibility." Maybe that's why I love creativity. It's inspiring to look at a pile of fabric and see a beautiful quilt in it, and maybe a set of pillowcases and a bag too. The possibilities are endless. No matter what life brings, there is always something we can do to find joy in each day.

Jenny

JENNY DOAN
MISSOURI STAR QUILT CO

TRY OUR APP

It's easy to keep up on every issue of BLOCK magazine. Access it from all your devices. And when you subscribe to BLOCK, it's free with your subscription! For the app, search BLOCK magazine in the app store. Available for both Apple and Android.

baskets
of blooms

The changing seasons are so full of symbolism. Watching the earth turn cold and desolate each winter followed by the rebirth of spring is a powerful lesson in hope, one that my friend Porter learned at a very young age.

Porter was just three years old when his father asked, "Hey buddy, would you like to come pick out a new tree for our front yard?" Porter jumped at any chance to ride in Daddy's big truck, and this day was no exception. At the nursery, they walked along rows and rows of saplings: maples, peaches, and pears. Finally, they stopped in front of a young flowering crabapple. It was seven feet tall with a nice, straight trunk and an even display of branches. "I like this baby tree best, Daddy!" And that was that. The little tree was loaded into the back of the pickup and home they went.

When they pulled into the driveway, Daddy got out his gloves and a shovel and went to work. Porter fetched his big green dump truck and a little blue shovel and went to work, too. Daddy dug big scoops of dirt and set them aside. Porter dug itty bitty scoops and piled them into his dump truck. It was hard work.

When the hole was just the right size, Daddy lowered the tree into place and Porter helped cover the root ball with the dirt from his dump truck. "I'm going to name my baby tree Branch." he exclaimed as he marched in a little circle all the way around the

trunk to pack the dirt down tight. They gave the tree a big drink of water just as the sun was going down. "Goodnight, Branch! Sleep tight!" called Porter as he went inside to put on his pajamas.

The next morning, Porter jumped out of bed and ran to the window to check on his baby tree. His face fell. "It looks lonely," he sighed. A robin flew by and rested on one of the little tree's branches. "Look, Mommy! Branch made a friend!"

All summer long, Porter watched out for his little tree. In the fall, the leaves turned a brilliant shade of golden yellow, and Porter could not have been more proud. But when winter

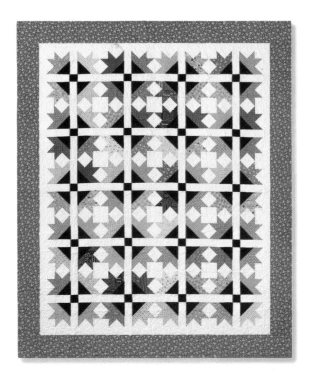

arrived, he started to worry. Icy winds blew relentlessly through those delicate, bare branches. After weeks and weeks of frightfully cold weather, the tree looked dead. "Don't worry, sweet boy." His mother snuggled him close. "You'll see. In the springtime your little Branch will be covered in flowers!"

So with all the patience his little three-year-old heart could muster, Porter waited for spring. Day after day, he checked for flowers. Day after day, he was disappointed. Until one April morning, when a single white bloom appeared. Before long, Porter's baby tree was bursting with life.

The seasons passed quickly, and suddenly it was winter once again. But this time, Porter wasn't worried. With all the wisdom of a four-year-old expert he smiled, "Don't worry! Branch will be just fine! And in the spring, he'll be covered in flowers."

materials

QUILT SIZE
71" x 85"

BLOCK SIZE
14" finished

QUILT TOP
1 roll of 2½" strips
3½ yards background fabric
   - includes inner border
1¼ yards complementary fabric

OUTER BORDER
1½ yards

BINDING
¾ yard

BACKING
5¼ yards - vertical seam(s)

SAMPLE QUILT
Farm Girl Vintage by Lori Holt of Bee in
my Bonnet for Riley Blake Designs

1 cut

From each 2½" print strip, cut:

- (2) 2½" squares, (4) 2½" x 4½"
  rectangles, and (2) 2½" x 6½"
  rectangles. Keep all matching
  prints together and stack the
  pieces into sets with each set
  made up of (1) 2½" square, (2)
  2½" x 4½" rectangles and (1)
  2½" x 6½" rectangle.

From the background fabric, cut:

- (39) 2½" strips across the
  width of the fabric – subcut
  each of 25 strips into 2½"
  squares. Each strip will yield

16 squares and a **total of 400**
are needed. Subcut each of 14
strips into 2½" x 6½" rectangles.
Each strip will yield 6 rectangles
and a **total of 80** are needed.

Set aside the remainder of the
background fabric for the
inner border.

From the complementary fabric, cut:

- (8) 4" strips across the width
  of the fabric – subcut the strips
  into 4" squares. Each strip will
  yield 10 squares and a **total of
  80** are needed.

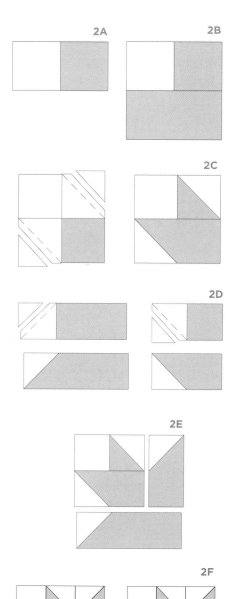

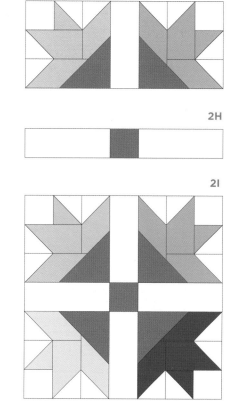

Draw a line from corner to corner once on the diagonal on the reverse side of (4) 2½" background squares.

Snowball 2 corners by placing a marked 2½" background square atop the unit with right sides facing as shown. Stitch on the drawn line. Trim the excess fabric ¼" away from the sewn seam. **2C**

Snowball a 2½" x 4½" print rectangle and a 2½" x 6½" print rectangle by sewing a 2½" marked background square to one end of each rectangle. Sew on the drawn line and trim as before. Sew the rectangles to the unit as shown. **2D, 2E**

Draw a line from corner to corner once on the diagonal on the reverse side of a 4" complementary square. Place the square atop the unit with right sides facing and sew on the drawn line. Trim ¼" away from the sewn seam. **2F**

Make 4 corner units using a different set of matching strips for each.

Sew a corner unit to either side of a 2½" x 6½" background rectangle. **Make 2. 2G**

Sew a 2½" x 6½" background rectangle to either side of a 2½" complementary square. **2H**

Sew the 3 rows together to complete 1 block. **Make 20. 2I**

Block Size: 14" finished

- (2) 2½" strips across the width of the fabric – subcut each strip into 2½" squares. Each strip will yield 16 squares and a **total of 20** are needed.

2 block construction
Pick up 4 different sets of 2½" strips.

To make a corner unit, sew a 2½" print square to a 2½" background square. **2A**

Add a 2½" x 4½" print rectangle as shown. **2B**

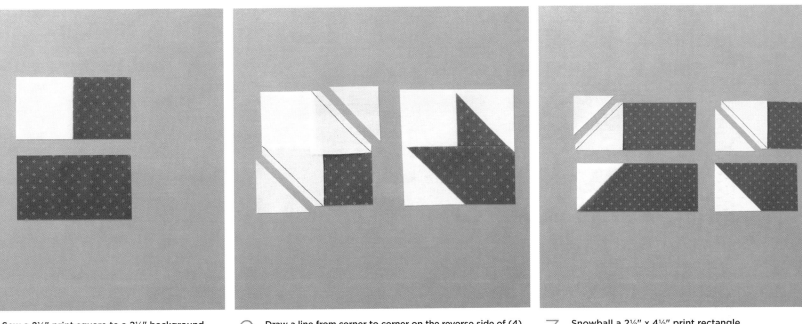

1 Sew a 2½″ print square to a 2½″ background square. Add a 2½″ x 4½″ matching print rectangle as shown.

2 Draw a line from corner to corner on the reverse side of (4) 2½″ background squares. Snowball 2 corners of the unit by placing a marked 2½″ background square atop the unit with right sides facing as shown. Sew on the drawn line. Trim the excess fabric away ¼″ from the sewn seam.

3 Snowball a 2½″ x 4½″ print rectangle and a 2½″ x 6½″ print rectangle by sewing a 2½″ marked square to one end of each rectangle with right sides facing. Sew on the drawn line and trim as before.

4 Sew the snowballed rectangles to the unit as shown.

5 Draw a line once on the diagonal on the reverse side of a 4″ complementary square. Place the marked square atop the unit with right sides facing as shown. Sew on the drawn line, then trim ¼″ away from the sewn seam. Make 4 corner units using a different set of matching strips for each.

6 Sew a corner unit to either side of a 2½″ x 6½″ background rectangle. Make 2. Sew a 2½″ x 6½″ background to either side of a 2½″ complementary square. Sew the 3 rows together to complete 1 block. Make 20.

3 arrange and sew

Lay out the blocks in rows. Each row is made up of **4 blocks** and **5 rows** are needed. After the blocks have been sewn into rows, press the seam allowances of the odd-numbered rows toward the right and the even-numbered rows toward the left to make the seams "nest."

Sew the rows together to complete the center of the quilt.

4 inner border

Cut (7) 2½" strips across the width of the fabric. Sew the strips together end-to-end to make one long strip. Trim the borders from this strip.

Refer to Borders (pg. 102) in the Construction Basics to measure and cut the inner borders. The strips are approximately 70½" for the sides and approximately 60½" for the top and bottom.

5 outer border

Cut (8) 6" strips across the width of the fabric. Sew the strips together end-to-end to make one long strip. Trim the borders from this strip.

Refer to Borders (pg. 102) in the Construction Basics to measure and cut the outer borders. The strips are approximately 74½" for the sides and approximately 71½" for the top and bottom.

6 quilt and bind

Layer the quilt with batting and backing and quilt. After the quilting is complete, square up the quilt and trim away all excess batting and backing. Add binding to complete the quilt. See Construction Basics (pg. 102) for binding instructions.

For the tutorial and everything you need to make this quilt visit:
www.msqc.co/blockearlywinter18

candy
twist

If I were lost in the woods and came upon a candy-covered gingerbread house, all my survival instincts would go out the window and I'd definitely be captured by a witch for nibbling on a bit of her home. I wouldn't be able to help myself! Gingerbread cookies are a winter favorite for my family with their sweet, spicy crunch.

My daughter, Sarah, has a fantastic mother-in-law who hosts a gingerbread house decorating night with more than 50 of her grandchildren every year. It has been a tradition in her home for over 20 years! She pulls out all the stops and the entire table is covered with bowls of candy for decorating. They have the traditional striped peppermints and candy canes, ribbon candy, oodles of gumdrops, cinnamon imperials, red ropes, and colorful wafers for the roof. Pretzels are great for fences and window panes too.

By the end of the night, all the grandchildren will have created an entire village of gingerbread houses that fill practically every surface in the house. Each gingerbread creation is unique and fun! It's amazing to see what the kids come up with. It's a crowded, loud, good time for everyone filled with plenty of sugar, and the kids all feel like a million bucks showing off their creations for the family.

Up in New York there's a man named Jon Lovitch who could give this family a run for their money. Just last year, he created an entire gingerbread village with a record number of tiny dwellings: 1,251 according to Guinness World Records. Can you imagine how much candy he used? And, believe it or not, Jon's held this record four times. I can definitely appreciate his dedication to gingerbread architecture.

Down in Texas, where big takes on a whole new meaning, the Traditions Club at Texas A&M University accomplished the feat of building the largest gingerbread house in the world a few years ago. This confectionery giant could literally house a family at 21 feet high and 2,520 square feet! But you might not want to take a bite. The recipe had been modified for strength and included 1,800 pounds of butter, 2,925 pounds of brown sugar, 7,200 eggs, 7,200 pounds of all-purpose flour, and 1,080 ounces of ground ginger. We think our recipe will taste a bit better. Go ahead and try it!

Classic Gingerbread Cookies

1 cup white sugar	6 cups flour
1 cup molasses	1 tsp. baking soda
¾ cup butter (1½ sticks)	½ tsp. salt
½ cup hot water	1 tsp. ground cinnamon
2 eggs	1½ tsp. ground ginger

DIRECTIONS

Mix the sugar, molasses, butter, and hot water together until smooth, then stir in the eggs. In a separate bowl combine the flour, baking soda, salt, cinnamon, and ginger, then stir into the wet ingredients to make a soft dough. Refrigerate dough for at least 1 hour until firm.

Roll out the cookie dough to ¼" thick on a floured surface. Cut into shapes using floured cookie cutters. Place cookies onto ungreased cookie sheets and bake for 10 minutes at 350° until the center is dry. Makes approx. 6 dozen cookies.

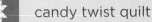

materials

QUILT SIZE
70″ x 79½″

BLOCK SIZE
9½″ finished

QUILT TOP
2 packages of 5″ print squares
1 package of 5″ background squares
4 yards background fabric
  - includes innermost and
    outermost borders

PIECED BORDER
¼ yard complementary fabric

BINDING
¾ yard

BACKING
5 yards - vertical seam(s)

SAMPLE QUILT
Adeline by Kathy Hall for Andover Fabrics

1 cut

From the background fabric, cut:

- (28) 3″ strips across the width of the fabric – subcut 17 strips into 3″ x 7½″ rectangles. Each strip will yield **5 rectangles** and a **total of 84** are needed. Subcut the remaining strips into 3″ x 5″ rectangles. Each strip will yield **8 rectangles** and a **total of 84** are needed.

- (6) 2½″ strips across the width of the fabric – subcut the strips into 2½″ squares. Each strip will yield **16 squares** and a **total of 84** are needed. You'll have 12 squares left over to use in another project. Set aside the remaining fabric for the innermost and outermost borders.

2 snowball 5″ squares

On the reverse side of each 2½″ background square, mark a line from corner to corner once on the diagonal. Place a marked background square on the upper right corner of a 5″ print square. Sew on the drawn line, then trim the excess fabric away ¼″ from the sewn seam. Repeat and sew another marked background square to the lower left corner. Trim as before. Press the seam allowances toward the darker fabric. **Make 42. 2A**

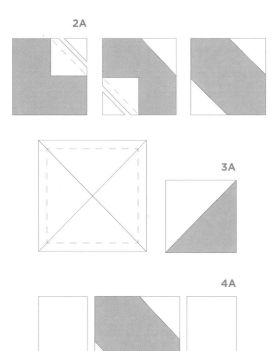

2A

3A

4A

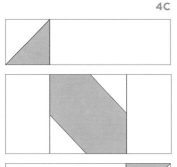

4B

4C

3 make half-square triangles

Layer a 5" print square with a 5" background square with right sides facing. Sew all the way around the perimeter using a ¼" seam allowance. Cut the sewn squares from corner to corner twice on the diagonal. Open and press the seam allowance toward the darker fabric. Each set of sewn squares will yield 4 half-square triangles for a **total of 164.** Stack all matching half-square triangles together and square each up to 3". **3A**

Note: 84 half-square triangle units will be used when making the blocks. The remaining units will be used in the pieced border.

4 block construction

To make the center unit of the block, sew a 3" x 5" background rectangle to either side of a snowballed square. **4A**

Pick up 2 half-square triangle units that match the snowballed square. Sew a half-square triangle unit to 1 end of a 3" x 7½" background rectangle. **Make 2. 4B**

Sew a rectangle to the top and bottom of the center unit to complete the block. **Make 42. 4C**

Block Size: 9½" finished

5 arrange and sew

Lay out the blocks in rows. Each row is made up of **6 blocks** and **7 rows** are needed. After the blocks have been sewn into rows, press the seam allowances of the odd-numbered rows toward the right and the even-numbered rows toward the left to make the seams "nest."

Sew the rows together to complete the center of the quilt.

6 innermost border

Cut (7) 2½" strips across the width of the fabric. Sew the strips together end-to-end to make one long strip. Trim the borders from this strip.

Refer to Borders (pg. 102) in the Construction Basics to measure and cut the innermost borders. The strips are approximately 67" for the sides and approximately 61½" for the top and bottom.

7 pieced border

Measure the quilt vertically through the center in several places. Average the numbers and sew enough half-square triangles together to equal your numbers. Each side should average about 71" and you will need

7A

7B

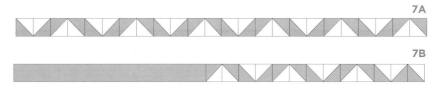

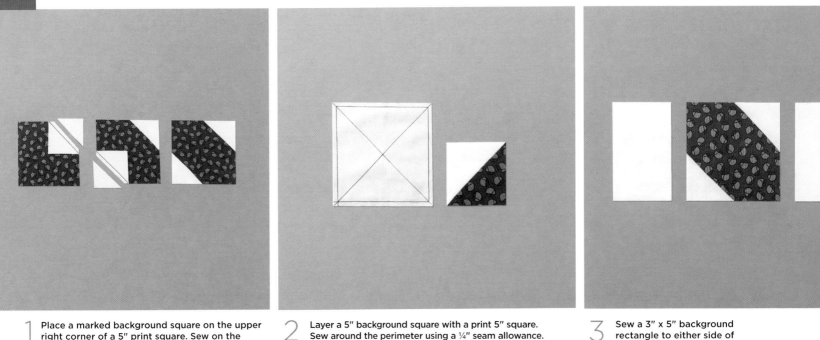

1 Place a marked background square on the upper right corner of a 5″ print square. Sew on the drawn line, then trim the excess fabric away ¼″ from sewn seam. Repeat and sew another marked background square to the lower left corner. Trim as before.

2 Layer a 5″ background square with a print 5″ square. Sew around the perimeter using a ¼″ seam allowance. Cut the sewn squares from corner to corner twice on the diagonal. Open and press. Square up each half-square triangle unit to 3″.

3 Sew a 3″ x 5″ background rectangle to either side of a snowballed square.

4 Sew a matching half-square triangle unit to 1 end of a 3″ x 7½″ background rectangle. Make 2.

5 Sew a rectangle unit to the top and bottom of the center unit as shown to complete the block. Make 42.

20

27 half-square triangle units. Refer to the diagram on page 19 and notice how the units are sewn together. Make 2 borders to your measurement and sew one to each side of the quilt.

Note: if the pieced border doesn't quite match up to the center of the quilt, make adjustments by using a larger or smaller seam allowance when sewing the half-square triangles together. **7A**

After sewing on the pieced side borders, measure the quilt in several places horizontally. Average the measurements as before. Sew 13 half-square triangle units together. From the complementary fabric, cut (2) 3″ strips across the width of the fabric. Add 1 of the 3″ strips to the half-square triangle units and trim to your measurement. The strip should be approximately 66½″ long. **Make 2.** Sew one to the top of the quilt and one to the bottom. **7B**

8 outermost border

Cut (8) 2½″ strips across the width of the remaining background fabric. Sew the strips together end-to-end to make one long strip. Trim the borders from this strip.

Refer to Borders (pg. 102) in the Construction Basics to measure and cut the outermost borders. The strips are approximately 76″ for the sides and approximately 70½″ for the top and bottom.

9 quilt and bind

Layer the quilt with batting and backing and quilt. After the quilting is complete, square up the quilt and trim away all excess batting and backing. Add binding to complete the quilt. See Construction Basics (pg. 102) for binding instructions.

bonus project
candy twist
table runner

SIZE
9½" x 66½"

BLOCK SIZE
9½" finished

TABLE RUNNER TOP
(12) 5" print squares
¾ yard background fabric

BINDING
½ yard

BACKING
1 yard - vertical seam(s)

SAMPLE FABRIC
Kona Cotton 30's palette and **Kona Snow** for Robert Kaufman Fabrics

1 cut

From the background fabric, cut:

- (1) 2½" strip across the width of the fabric. Subcut the strip into (12) 2½" squares.

- (1) 5" strip across the width of the fabric. Subcut the strip into (6) 5" squares.

- (2) 3" strips across the width of the fabric. Subcut 1 strip into (8) 3" x 5" rectangles and cut (4) 3" x 5" rectangles from the other strip.

- (1) 10" strip across the width of the fabric. Subcut (1) 10" square from the strip and set aside to use as the center block in the runner. There will be a piece left that measures at least 10" x 30".

From that strip cut:

- (3) 3" strips across the width of the piece. Subcut each strip into (4) 3" x 7½" rectangles.

2 make block units

Follow the directions on page 18 and snowball (6) 5" squares. Set them aside while you make half-square triangles using the same directions as found on page 19. You need a **total of 12 half-square triangles**.

Refer to the Block Construction directions on page 19 and make 6 blocks.

3 arrange and sew

Sew 3 blocks to either side of the 10" background square. See the diagram to the right.

4 quilt and bind

Layer the backing, batting and top of the runner and quilt. After the quilting is complete, square up the runner and trim away all excess batting and backing. Add binding to compete the table runner. See Construction Basics (pg. 102) for binding instructions.

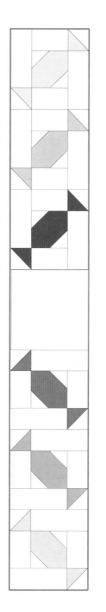

little stitches

Can you imagine what quilting would be like if it were an Olympic sport? I can picture it now— the yardage dash, freestyle rotary cutting, iron curling, speed stitching, the ironing board luge, a template triathlon, and much more. It would be the event of the year in my book! Well, until sewing becomes a sport, I'm happy to watch the athletes from the sidelines.

Two years ago, we took the entire family on a trip to Granby, Colorado. This sleepy town nestled in the Rockies is incredibly charming. I'd go back just to enjoy the majestic view of snow-capped mountains and sip hot cocoa by the fire with a stack of English paper piecing on my lap.

Now, I'm not much of a skier myself and neither is my husband, Ron. You may not know this, but almost ten years ago, while filming one of Missouri Star's first tutorials, I broke my leg! During the course of my life, I have broken both of my legs, so I won't be taking a trip down the slopes anytime soon.

Granby is known for snowmobiling, ice fishing, dog sledding, and snowshoeing, but especially skiing. In our family, some are skiers and snowboarders, and some have never even strapped on a pair of skis in their lives, but when we went to Granby we

For the tutorial and everything you need to make this quilt visit:
www.msqc.co/blockearlywinter18

all had a blast together. It was a lot of fun seeing all the grandkids bundled up in their bright jackets and scarves on the bunny hill, slowly making their way down the mountain. Those brave kids amazed me! By the end of the day, many of them were taking on the big hills alongside their parents.

I had a quilting cruise coming up that I definitely didn't want to miss due to any broken bones, so I opted to do some sewing while I cheered on Ron and the kids. He

did his best to stay upright, but kept falling over again and again. After a while, the grandkids, who had gained some confidence on the bunny hill, came to his rescue and helped him out. With their coaching, he was able to finally stand up on his skis!

It was sweet to watch it all unfold. I think it's great for the grandkids (and their grandpa) to remember that they don't know it all and that everything is a learned skill. No matter where you begin, you can always improve. That's one of my favorite mantras. Just keep trying and you'll be amazed at what you can do.

materials

WALL HANGING SIZE
36" x 49½" finished

BLOCK SIZE
4½" finished

WALL HANGING TOP
1 package 5" print squares
½ yard background fabric
¼ yard complementary fabric

BORDER
¾ yard

BINDING
½ yard

BACKING
1¾ yards

OTHER MATERIALS
½ yard lightweight fusible web

SAMPLE QUILT
Scribbles Single Scoops by
Andover Fabrics

1 sew

Lay out the 5" print squares in **7 rows**
of **6 squares**, mixing up the light,
medium and dark colors. When you
are happy with the appearance, sew
the squares into rows. Press the seam
allowances of the odd rows toward the
left and the even rows toward the right
to make the seams "nest."

Sew **6 rows** together. Reserve the
remaining row for the top of the quilt.

From the background fabric, cut a
13" x 27½" rectangle.

Note: if you like, you can cut the
rectangle wider, then trim the edges
the same width as the sewn rows.

Place the background rectangle on
top of the sewn squares with the right
side up on both pieces. The end of the
rectangle should overlap the first row of
squares just enough to allow you to cut
the curve. You may be able to see the
row of squares shadowing through the
background piece so you can tell how
much room you have as you cut. Pin the
rectangle in place. **1A**

Using a rotary cutter, freehand cut a
gentle curve similar to the one shown
in the photo on page 26. Notice how
the curve dips into the sewn row of
squares in several places. Keep in mind
that there is no "wrong" way to cut the
curve! **1B**

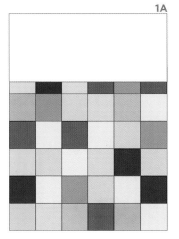

1A

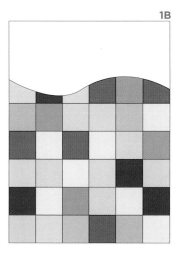

1B

1C

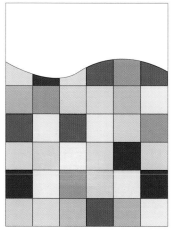

Pin the two pieces together along the curved edge with right sides facing. Sew the two pieces together along the curve using a ¼" seam allowance. Open and press the seams toward the sewn rows. Square up the top to 27½" x 36½".

Add the remaining row of sewn squares to the top. **1C**

2 fuse and appliqué

Place the fusible web over the templates for the needle and scissors with the paper side up. Trace the templates onto the paper. Fuse the web onto the reverse side of the complimentary color you've chosen and cut out the pieces.

Note: we've already reversed the pieces on the templates so they will be oriented the same as you see them on the quilt after fusing in place.

Add fusible to the reverse side of a ½" strip of your chosen color. Cut the strip into increments that are approximately 1¼" long. We used 13 pieces for the stitches.

Place the appliqué pieces onto the background piece in a whimsical fashion, using the diagram on page 31 as a guide. Don't worry about being exact!

Fuse the pieces in place following the directions given for the brand of fusible web you're using. Stitch around the pieces using a buttonhole stitch or a small zigzag.

3 border

Cut (4) 5" strips across the width of the fabric. Sew the strips together end-to-end to make one long strip. Trim the borders from this strip.

Refer to Borders (pg. 102) in the Construction Basics to measure and cut the outer borders. The strips are approximately 41" for the sides and approximately 36½" for the top and bottom.

4 quilt and bind

Layer the wall hanging with batting and backing and quilt. After the quilting is complete, square up the quilt and trim away all excess batting and backing. Add binding to complete the quilt. See Construction Basics (pg. 102) for binding instructions.

Templates are 100% and have been reversed for your convenience.

1 After sewing rows together, place the background rectangle on top of the sewn squares with the right side facing up on both pieces. The end of the rectangle should overlap the first row of squares just enough to allow you to cut the curve. Use a rotary cutter to freehand cut a gentle curve.

2 Pin the two pieces together with right sides facing. Sew the 2 pieces together along the curve using a ¼" seam allowance.

3 Add the remaining row of sewn 5" squares to the top.

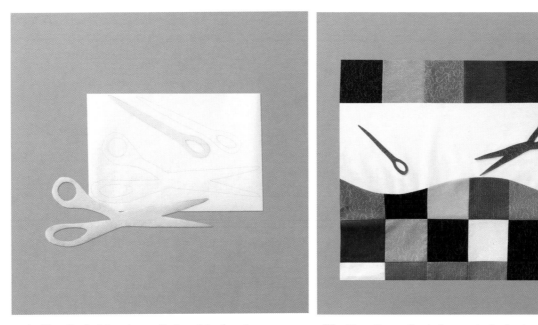

4 Place the fusible web over the templates found on pages 29 and 31 with the paper side up. Trace the templates onto the paper. Fuse the web onto the reverse side of the fabric you've chosen and cut out the pieces.

5 Place the appliqué pieces onto the background piece in a whimsical fashion using the diagram on page 31 as a guide. Add the rectangles that represent the stitches and stitch around the pieces using a buttonhole stitch or a small zigzag.

Templates are
100% and have been
reversed for your
convenience.

For the tutorial and everything
you need to make this quilt visit:
www.msqc.co/blockearlywinter18

pinwheel
picnic

For me, the best time to go camping is right as the cool fall weather settles in; not too hot, not too cold, and you're surrounded by beautiful scenery. For some Boy Scout troops, however, camping is a year-round activity. My friend's son, Richard, belonged to such a troop as a young teen, and they reveled in cold-weather camping! There's even a competition held in our neck of the woods for Scouts called the Klondike Derby, and Richard was excited to attend his very first winter outing. Little did he know, that particular January weekend would be one of the coldest in Missouri history.

The Klondike Derby is held at Camp Geiger, just north of St. Joseph along the bluffs of the Missouri River. It's a friendly, but intense, competition between the local Scout troops as they practice winter survival skills and techniques to see which troop is the fastest, most resourceful, and most prepared for cold-weather survival. Richard and his friends had spent weeks practicing their skills so they would have a chance to show up rival troops.

After all the Scouts had arrived, the Scoutmasters began the first day of competitions. Amid freshly fallen snow, Richard's group was able to use their home-built Iditarod-style wooden sled to race to victory in the sled races. They also set a record for the fastest firebuilding in the campfire contest! Spirits were

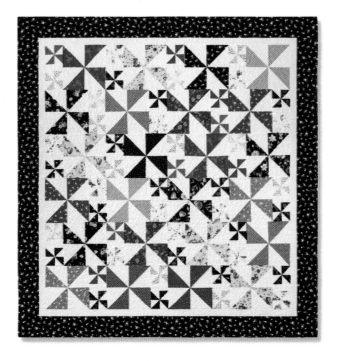

running high as Richard's troop sped through the events like a well-oiled machine. While they didn't place first in the igloo building competition, they were still in the lead as the sun set over the frost-rimmed Missouri River.

However, the real challenge was still in store for the Scouts. As nighttime descended, a chilling wind blew in from the north. Over the next few hours, the temperature plummeted 30°! Richard could hear ice cracking as the river quickly froze over. The Scouts' teeth chattered as they lay restlessly in their sleeping bags.

By morning, Richard felt he had more in common with a popsicle than a Boy Scout! But a new day of competition awaited. So, they all bundled up and trudged on through the snow, determined to win. The troop performed well, despite their shivering, and they ended up placing first! The boys were excited, but could barely summon the energy to celebrate. After a shortened awards ceremony, an announcement was made that the second night of camping was canceled, as the forecast called for temperatures to drop to -30°! The relieved Scouts were promptly taken home to defrost. As for Richard, he went straight to his room, bundled up under the heaviest quilt he had, and didn't come out until it was time for school on Monday morning!

Now that some years have passed, Richard admits, although he enjoyed the adventure he had that icy January weekend, you'll never see him out camping past October! It seems he may have learned the most important winter survival rule of them all: Don't get caught out in the cold in the first place!

materials

QUILT SIZE
83" X 87"

BLOCK SIZE
17" x 12" finished

QUILT TOP
1 package 10" print squares
1 package 10" background squares
1 yard of background fabric
  - includes inner border

OUTER BORDER
1½ yards

BINDING
¾ yard

BACKING
8 yards - vertical seam(s)
  or 2¾ yards 108" wide

SAMPLE QUILT
Afternoon Picnic by Nancy Zieman
Productions for Penny Rose Fabrics

1 cut

From the background yardage, cut:

- (12) 2½" strips across the width of the fabric – subcut 4 strips into 2½" x 5½" rectangles. Each strip will yield 7 rectangles and a **total of 24** are needed. Set aside the remainder of the strips for the inner border.

2 large half-square triangles

Select 24 print 10" squares. Layer each with a background 10" square with right sides facing. Sew all around the perimeter of the layered squares using a ¼" seam

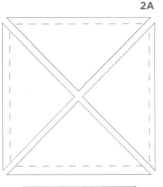

2A

36

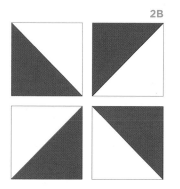

2B

allowance. Cut the sewn squares from corner to corner twice on the diagonal. Open each section to reveal a half-square triangle unit. Press the seam allowance toward the darker fabric and square each to 6½". **2A**

Sew 4 half-square triangles together as shown to make a pinwheel. **Make 24** and set aside for the moment. **2B**

3 small half-square triangles

Select 12 print 10" squares and 12 background 10" squares. Cut each square into (4) 5" squares.

Layer a print 5" square with a background 5" square with right sides facing. Sew all around the perimeter of the layered squares using a ¼" seam allowance. Cut the sewn squares from corner to corner twice on the diagonal. Open each section to reveal a half-square triangle unit. Press the seam allowance toward the darker fabric and square each to 3". Refer to diagram **2A**.

Sew 4 half-square triangles together as shown to make a pinwheel. **Make 48** and set aside for the moment. **2B**

4 block construction

Sew a small pinwheel to either side of a 2½" x 5½" background rectangle. **4A**

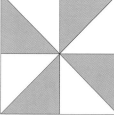

4A

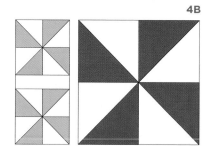

4B

Sew a large pinwheel to the side of the sewn small pinwheels to complete the block. **Make 24 blocks. 4B**

Block Size: 17" x 12"

5 arrange and sew

Lay out the blocks in rows. Each row is made up of **4 blocks** across and **6 rows** are needed. Sew the blocks together into rows. **Make 3 rows** that begin with the small pinwheels on the left and **3 rows** that begin with the large pinwheel on the left. Refer to the diagram on page 39, if necessary. Sew the rows together to complete the center of the quilt.

6 inner border

Pick up the (8) 2½" background strips you put aside earlier. Sew the strips together end-to-end to make one long strip. Trim the borders from this strip.

Refer to Borders (pg. 102) in the Construction Basics to measure and cut the inner borders. The strips are approximately 72½" for the sides and approximately 72½" for the top and bottom.

7 outer border

Cut (8) 6" strips across the width of the fabric. Sew the strips together end-to-end to make one long strip. Trim the borders from this strip.

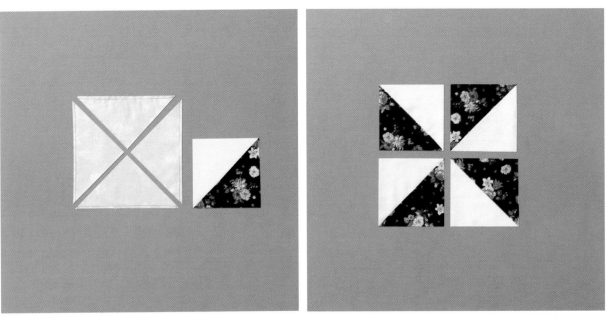

1 Layer a background 10″ square with a print 10″ square. Sew all around the perimeter using a ¼″ seam allowance. Cut the sewn squares from corner to corner twice on the diagonal. Open each section to reveal a half-square triangle unit. Square each to 6½″.

2 Sew 4 large half-square triangles together as shown to make a large pinwheel.

3 Sew a small pinwheel to either side of a 2½″ x 5½″ background rectangle.

4 Stitch the small pinwheel unit to the large pinwheel to complete the block. Make 24.

Refer to Borders (pg. 102) in the Construction Basics to measure and cut the outer borders. The strips are approximately 76½" for the sides and approximately 83½" for the top and bottom.

8 quilt and bind

Layer the quilt with batting and backing and quilt. After the quilting is complete, square up the quilt and trim away all excess batting and backing. Add binding to complete the quilt. See Construction Basics (pg. 102) for binding instructions.

scallop city

From Birthday Bash to Jenny on the Road, 2018 has been quite a journey! I like looking back over the highs and lows that we have had to give myself a moment to enjoy the success we've experienced and look for learning opportunities. Many positive things have happened and here's a rundown of some wonderful moments from the past year.

In May, Missouri Star was recognized by Forbes Magazine as a "Small Giant," one of the best small companies of the year. We joined the ranks of 25 other companies who were recognized for their community involvement, commitment to employees, and excellence in their industry. It was a wonderful accomplishment for a company that has grown from a tiny six-person operation to a thriving business in ten short years.

We held our second annual Missouri Star Academy and it was a great success. Hundreds of quilters came to town to find inspiration and learn from incredible teachers. They were taught about everything from organization and time-saving techniques to working with specialty fabrics and notions. It was a blast rubbing shoulders with designers we admire, making new friends, and beginning fun projects.

For the tutorial and everything you need to make this quilt visit:
www.msqc.co/blockearlywinter18

September 20th to the 22nd was Missouri Star's Birthday Bash for our 10th anniversary and we celebrated in a big way! Over 3,000 people came through town to enjoy the festivities, more than doubling the population of our hometown. The celebration included a kickoff dinner on two nights for 200 people each, the Ultimate Sewlebrity Sew-off, a charity sewing event benefiting Days for Girls, trunk shows, watercolor classes from Let's Make Art, and an incredible, professional fireworks show, the first of its kind in Hamilton in two decades!

Through these events, we were able to raise a record-breaking sum of over $5,000 for the Hamilton Food Pantry with raffle money from Missouri Star quilts, the Sewlebrity Sew-off, and the Great Missouri Star Vendor Bake-off, where vendors you know and love helped make fabric cakes and our guests bought tickets for a chance to win them! In addition to this, 730 female hygiene kits were made for Days for Girls.

Finally, our Fall Festival attracted quilters from near and far for an entire week of down-home comforts, designer presentations, exciting demos, meet and greets, activities, and a daily quilt show. They left feeling inspired and energized to start the quilting season off right.

I can't wait to see what the coming year will hold. It's humbling to be able to do what I love every day and, truly, it's only possible because of your support. Thanks for another wonderful year!

43

materials

QUILT SIZE
56" x 66"

BLOCK SIZE
6" x 4" finished

QUILT TOP
1 roll of 2½" print strips
1¼ yards background fabric
 - includes inner border

OUTER BORDER
1 yard

BINDING
¾ yard

BACKING
3½ yards - horizontal seam(s)

SAMPLE QUILT
Fruitful Pleasures by Lila Tueller
for Riley Blake Designs

1 cut

Select 29 strips from the roll. From each strip, cut:

- (6) 2½" x 4½" rectangles, (5) 2½" squares – subcut (2) 2½" squares into (4) 1¼" squares. Keep all matching prints together.

From the background fabric, cut:

- (6) 2½" strips across the width of the fabric - subcut each strip into 2½" squares. Each strip will yield 16 squares and a **total of 85** are needed.

- (6) 1¼" strips across the width of the fabric – subcut each strip into 1¼" squares. Each strip will yield 32 squares and a **total of 170** are needed.

- (2) 3½" strips across the width of the fabric – subcut each strip into 3½" x 4½" rectangles. Each strip will yield 8 rectangles and a **total of 12** are needed.

Set aside the remainder of the fabric for the inner border.

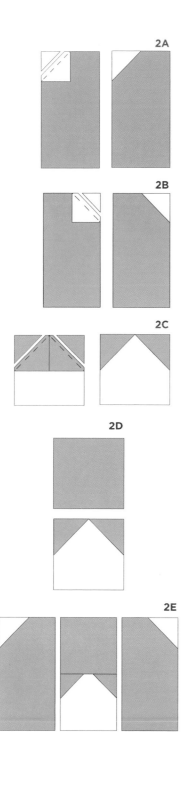

2A

2B

2C

2D

2E

2 block construction

Pick up 2 matching 2½" x 4½" print rectangles, 1 matching 2½" print square and 2 matching 1¼" print squares. Add a 2½" background square and (2) 1¼" background squares to the stack.

On the reverse side of each 1¼" square, draw a line from corner to corner once on the diagonal to mark a sewing line. If you'd rather not draw a line, just fold the square once on the diagonal and press a crease in place to mark a sewing line. *(You might just want to eyeball it because it's such a short distance.)*

Place a marked 1¼" background square atop the upper left corner of a 2½" x 4½" print rectangle. Sew on the marked line, then trim the excess fabric away ¼" from the sewn seam. **2A**

Place a marked 1¼" background square atop the upper right corner of a 2½" x 4½" print rectangle. Sew on the marked line, then trim the excess fabric away ¼" from the sewn seam. **2B**

Set those 2 rectangles aside for the moment.

Now place a marked 1¼" print square atop a 2½" background square with right sides facing. Sew on the marked line, then trim the excess fabric away ¼" from the sewn seam. Repeat for the other side of the background square. **2C**

Sew the snowballed 2½" background square to the 2½" print square. **2D**

Sew a snowballed 2½" x 4½" print rectangle to either side of sewn squares as shown to complete the block. **2E**

Make 85 blocks.
Block Size: 6" x 4" finished

3 arrange and sew

Arrange the blocks into rows. **Make 7 rows** using **7 blocks** across. **Make 6 rows** using **6 blocks** across. Add a 3½" x 4½" rectangle to each end of each short row. Sew the rows together, beginning with a full row of blocks, then add a row with 6 full blocks. Continue to alternate in this manner until all 13 rows have been sewn together to complete the center of the quilt. Refer to the diagram on page 47 if necessary.

4 inner border

Cut (5) 2½" strips across the width of the fabric. Sew the strips together end-to-end to make one long strip. Trim the borders from this strip.

Refer to Borders (pg. 102) in the Construction Basics to measure and cut the inner borders. The strips are

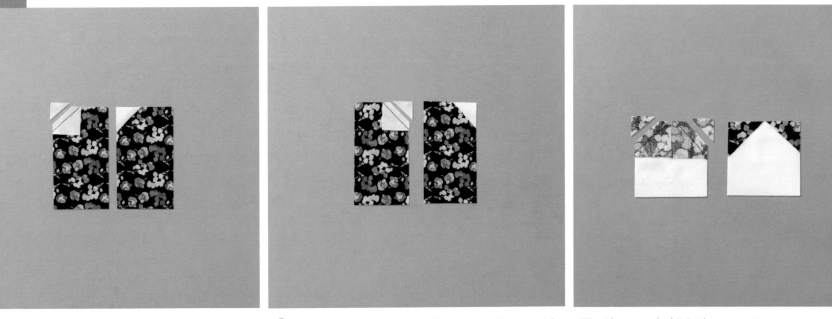

1 Place a marked 1¼" print square atop the upper left corner of a 2½" x 4½" print rectangle with right sides facing. Sew on the marked line, then trim the excess fabric away ¼" from the sewn seam. Open and press.

2 Place a marked 1¼" background square atop the upper right corner of matching 2½" x 4½" print rectangle. Sew on the marked line and trim as before.

3 Place a marked 1¼" print square atop a 2½" background square with right sides facing. Sew on the marked line, then trim the excess fabric away ¼" from the sewn seam. Repeat for the other side of the background square.

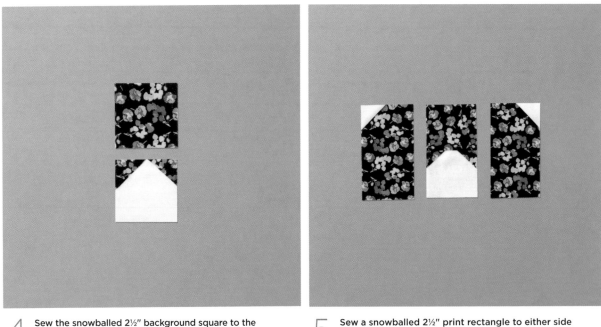

4 Sew the snowballed 2½" background square to the matching 2½" print square.

5 Sew a snowballed 2½" print rectangle to either side of the sewn squares as shown to complete the block. Make 85.

approximately 52½" for the sides and approximately 46½" for the top and bottom.

5 outer border

Cut (6) 5½" strips across the width of the fabric. Sew the strips together end-to-end to make one long strip. Trim the borders from this strip.

Refer to Borders (pg. 102) in the Construction Basics to measure and cut the outer borders. The strips are approximately 56½" for the sides and approximately 56½" for the top and bottom.

6 quilt and bind

Layer the quilt with batting and backing and quilt. After the quilting is complete, square up the quilt and trim away all excess batting and backing. Add binding to complete the quilt. See Construction Basics (pg. 102) for binding instructions.

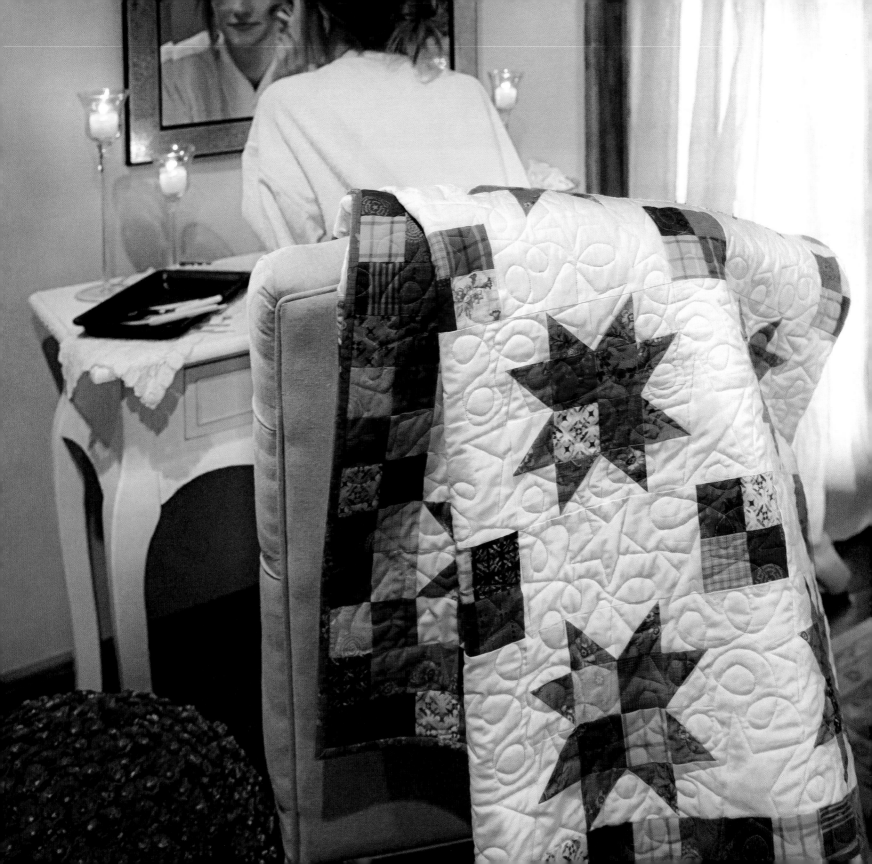

For the tutorial and everything
you need to make this quilt visit:
www.msqc.co/blockearlywinter18

star patch

The very first snowstorm of the season is magical. Everything is wrapped in a blanket of shimmering white, and it is beautiful, new, and oh so exciting! But as the winter months plod on, the novelty begins to fade. Waking up to a fresh layer of spring snow isn't nearly as much fun when you're wishing for tulips.

I've experienced a few springtime snowstorms here and there, but nothing compares to the snow-white wedding of my good friend Pam Wynne.

It was June 29, 1968, a day that, by all accounts, should have been as summery as they come, yet it felt more like January. The wind whipped in biting, bitter sprints, and the sky was dark and angry.

Looking through her wedding album, I noticed the portrait of Pam as a lovely, young bride. She is standing in front of the church in an empire waist gown with long sleeves and a high, ruffled collar. Her arms are folded across her chest and she is holding tight to the lacey edges of a floor-length veil that is trying it's best to fly away in the frost-filled wind. Her nose and cheeks are cherry red, and she wears an expression of comical despair. "It was either laugh or cry." Pam explained. "I did a bit of both."

It wasn't all the sort of day Pam had envisioned when she planned her garden reception. When she picked out the

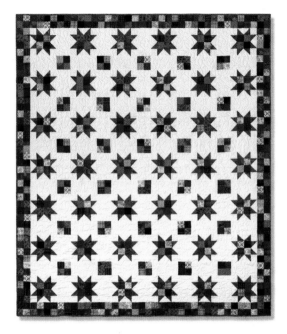

long, flowing dresses for her seven beautiful bridesmaids, she never dreamed they'd be hidden under heavy, woolen coats. And as she and her mother worked all spring to prepare the yard with rusty orange and gold marigolds to accent her on-trend color scheme, she never dreamed her wedding celebration would be relegated to the basement family room.

Friends and family who had braved the storm were clumped together on well-worn sofas and dining room chairs. Wedding gifts were stacked on the coffee table next to the TV Guide, and a three-tiered cake adorned with delicate icing daisies sat proudly in the middle of the pool table.

No, it wasn't the reception of her dreams, but as the night wore on, Pam looked around that basement living room and realized, it was filled to the brim with all her favorite people on earth, and she was determined to celebrate!

And so they laughed and danced and reminisced. The cake was cut, the bouquet tossed, and the happy couple bid farewell, although they had to do a bit of shoveling to get the car out of the driveway. And wouldn't you know, the next morning they awoke to blue sky and sunshine—and not a trace of snow to be seen!

This summer Pam and her husband will reach their 50th anniversary. Fifty years of babies and grandbabies. Fifty years of adventure and struggle and joy. But in all those fifty years there is one thing they've never again experienced: a snowstorm on June 29th!

materials

QUILT SIZE
76" x 88"

BLOCK SIZE
8" finished

QUILT TOP
1 roll of 2½" print strips
1½ yards complementary fabric
4½ yards background fabric

BINDING
¾ yard

BACKING
7 yards - horizontal seam(s)

SAMPLE QUILT
Tickled Pink by Janet Rae Nesbit
of One Sister Designs for Henry
Glass Fabrics

1 cut

From the complementary
fabric, cut:

- (21) 2½" strips across the width of
  the fabric – subcut each strip into
  2½" squares. Each strip will yield
  16 squares and a **total of 336** are
  needed.

From the background fabric, cut:

- (9) 8½" strips across the width of
  the fabric – subcut each strip into
  4½" x 8½" rectangles. Each strip will
  yield 8 rectangles and a **total of 71**
  are needed. Set aside for sashing.

- (32) 2½" strips across the width of
  the fabric – subcut each strip into
  2½" squares. Each strip will yield
  16 squares and a **total of 504** are
  needed.

2 sew

Sew 2 print 2½" strips together along
the length to make a strip set. **Make
19** and cut each strip set into (16) 2½"
x 4½" rectangles for a **total of (300)
2-patches. 2A**

Sew (2) 2-patches together as shown to
make a 4-patch. **Make a total of 150. 2B**

2A

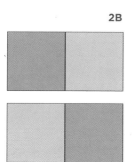

2B

3A

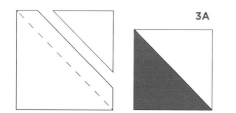

3B

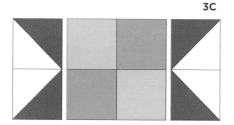

3C

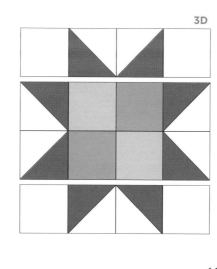

3D

4A

3 block construction

Pick up (8) 2½" squares cut from the complementary fabric as well as (12) 2½" background squares. Add a 4-patch unit to the stack.

Draw a line from corner to corner on the reverse side of (8) 2½" background squares. If you'd rather not be bothered drawing the line, just fold the square once on the diagonal with the right sides together and press a crease in place to mark your sewing line. Layer a 2½" background square with a 2½" complementary square with right sides facing. Sew on the marked line, then trim ¼" away from the sewn seam. **Make 8** star point units. **3A**

Sew 2 star point units together, then add a 2½" background square to either end to make rows 1 and 3. **3B**

Sew 2 star point units together. Add 1 to either side of a 4-patch to make the center row. **3C**

Sew the 3 rows together to complete the block. **3D Make 42.**

Block Size: 8" finished

4 arrange and sew

Lay out the blocks in rows with each row made up of **6 blocks.** Alternate each block with a 4½" x 8½" sashing rectangle. **Make 7 rows.**

Make a horizontal sashing strip by sewing 4-patches and sashing rectangles together. Begin with a sashing rectangle, then add a 4-patch. Continue on in this manner until you have sewn a row that has 6 sashing rectangles and (5) 4-patches. **Make 6. 4A**

Sew the rows together, adding a horizontal sashing strip between each to complete the center of the quilt.

5 border

Measure the center of the quilt in 2 or 3 places vertically. Average the 3 numbers to determine the length of the quilt. It should be approximately 80½". Sew enough 4-patches together to equal your measurement (approximately 20). If your border doesn't quite fit, use a scant ¼" seam allowance in some of the 4-patches

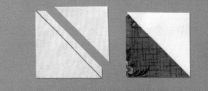

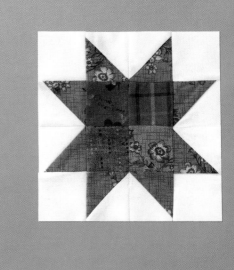

1 Sew 2 print 2½" strips together along the length to make a strip set. Make 19 and cut each strip set into (16) 2½" x 4½" rectangles.

2 Sew (2) 2-patch pieces together to make a 4-patch.

3 Draw a line from corner to corner once on the diagonal on the reverse side of (8) 2½" background squares. Layer a marked background square with a complementary square with right sides facing. Sew on the marked line, trim ¼" away from the sewn seam. Make 8 star point units.

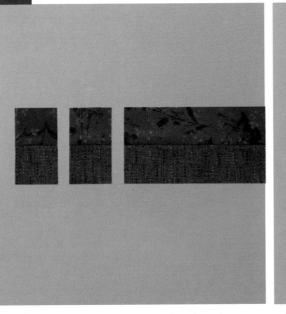

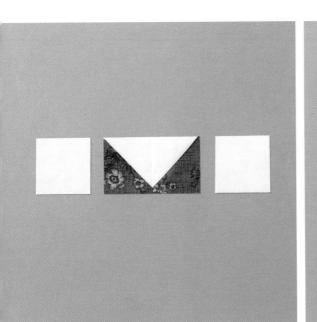

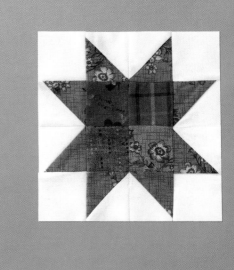

4 Sew 2 star point units together. Add a 2½" background square to either end to make rows 1 and 3.

5 Sew 2 star point units together. Make 2 and sew one to either side of a 4-patch unit to make the center row.

6 Sew the 3 rows together to complete 1 block. Make 42.

until the border is adjusted to fit. **Make 2** and sew a border to each side of the quilt.

Measure the center of the quilt horizontally in several places. Add the measurements and average them to determine the width of the quilt. Remember, you need to include the borders you have already sewn to each side of the quilt. It should measure approximately 76½". Sew enough 4-patches together to equal your measurement (approximately 19). Adjust the border just like you did for the sides, if necessary. **Make 2** and sew one to the top of the quilt and one to the bottom.

6 quilt and bind

Layer the quilt with batting and backing and quilt. After the quilting is complete, square up the quilt and trim away all excess batting and backing. Add binding to complete the quilt. See Construction Basics (pg. 102) for binding instructions.

sundance

By Rob Appell

Growing up near the beaches of California, I never experienced changing seasons. I would see more wind on the ocean in the springtime and bigger waves in the winter, but I could usually count on sunny days. As I've gotten older, I see the beauty in shifting seasons and I'm learning to welcome change, whether it be in the world around me or in my life.

Coming to Hamilton to teach is always an interesting experience. It couldn't be more different from California, but it's refreshing. Every time I visit, it looks different. Sometimes it's snowy, other times it's covered in fallen leaves, and there's nothing like a warm spring day in town. Experiencing changing seasons hasn't always been a comfortable experience for me, however.

Seasonal changes initially caused me some worry, but then I learned to take a deep breath and think "This too shall pass." I love summertime because I love sunlight. I enjoy being up at six in the summer when it's already light outside. So, in the depths of winter, I need to keep reminding myself that seasons do change. The same goes for life. I often find myself bouncing from one idea to the other because I'm always looking forward to the next fun thing.

Man Sewing gives me many opportunities to dash from one awesome adventure to another, but I often feel lonely and

tired on the road. Within one day I can go from one high to another low because I encounter so many new and unexpected experiences as I travel. Don't get me wrong, I thoroughly love interacting with fellow quilters wherever I go. They are so kind and treat me so well. They share such personal, touching experiences and I often carry those feelings with me. I'm glad that they find healing in creativity, as I have myself.

Last year, I became depressed—it felt like I was on an emotional roller coaster. It's difficult to be creative when you just want to curl up and cry. As a guy, I'm not supposed to want to cry. So, I hired another guy I could cry with. I started seeing a counselor, and he quickly pointed out that I'm simply in a new season of life. These seasons come and go, but it's up to me to adapt with them. In other words, if it's snowing outside, it's not a great day for shorts and flip flops.

Recently, a good friend of mine survived a wildfire that left devastation for miles surrounding his home. I wondered how the house was spared, but also I looked at the charred landscape and thought, would I still want to live there? Later on, I drove through an area where a wildfire had burned everything a few years back. Everything was still charcoal black from the fire, but I spotted new growth. The pines were small, but bright green. The purple lupine was blooming. Then I realized, we all have struggles in different seasons of our lives. Looking at the bigger picture shows us how important our struggles are as the seasons change us and strengthen us. The forest needs the fire for the rebirth, and even after the worst blaze, not all is lost. The flowers will return.

materials

QUILT SIZE
37" x 43"

BLOCK SIZE
6" finished

QUILT TOP
1 package of 5" print squares
1 package of 5" background squares

INNER BORDER
¼ yard

OUTER BORDER
¾ yard

BINDING
½ yard

BACKING
2½ yards - horizontal seam(s)

OTHER
1 Moda Cupcake Mix Recipe
Foundation Paper Pattern Pad #4

SAMPLE QUILT
Home Again by Jill Finley of Jillily
Studios for Penny Rose Fabrics

1 sew

Layer a print 5" square with a background 5" square. Make sure the background square is on top. Pin 1 foundation paper on the top. Shorten the stitch length on your sewing machine. Follow the arrows on the foundation pattern and stitch on the dotted lines. Cut on the solid lines. Each foundation paper makes ½ of a block so you'll need to use 2 foundations to complete 1 block.

Make 20. 1A

Block size: 6" finished

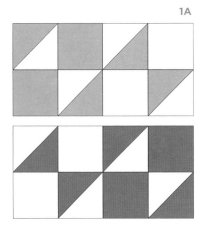

1A

2 arrange and sew

Lay out the blocks in rows. Refer to the diagram on page 63 and notice how the blocks are oriented. Each row is made up of **4 blocks** across and **5 rows** are needed. Sew the blocks together into rows. Press the seam allowances of the odd rows toward the right and the even rows toward the left to make the seams "nest."

3 inner border

Cut (3) 2½" strips from the fabric being used for the inner border. Sew the strips together end-to-end to make one long strip. Trim the borders from this strip.

Refer to Borders (pg. 102) in the Construction Basics to measure and cut the inner borders. The strips are approximately 30½" for the sides and approximately 28½" for the top and bottom.

4 outer border

Cut (4) 5" strips across the width of the fabric. Sew the strips together end-to-end to make one long strip. Trim the borders from this strip.

Refer to Borders (pg. 102) in the Construction Basics to measure and cut the outer borders. The strips are approximately 34½" for the sides and approximately 37½" for the top and bottom.

5 quilt and bind

Layer the quilt with batting and backing and quilt. After the quilting is complete, square up the quilt and trim away all excess batting and backing. Add binding to complete the quilt. See Construction Basics (pg. 102) for binding instructions.

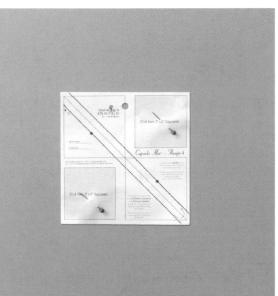

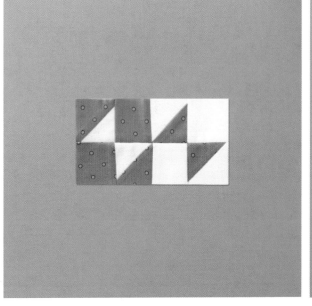

1 Layer a print 5″ square with a background 5″ square. Make sure the background square is on top. Pin 1 foundation paper on the top. Shorten the stitch length on the sewing machine. Follow the arrows on the foundation pattern and stitch on the dotted lines. Cut on the solid lines.

2 Follow the instructions on the foundation paper and sew the pieces together. Keep in mind that each foundation paper makes one half of a block.

3 Lay out 2 halves of the block, being aware of how each is oriented. Sew the 2 halves together to complete the block.

For the tutorial and everything you need to make this quilt visit:
www.msqc.co/blockearlywinter18

time to sew

As the new year approaches, do you feel that empowering rush of inspiration and start making a list of New Year's resolutions? Many of us do! We may stroll into the new year determined to complete every unfinished quilt, cut back on caffeine, read more books, or even learn to sew. Though there are, somewhere out there, rare and talented people who miraculously find the time to actually achieve their New Year's resolution, many of us get lost along the way. Why is that, and is there a way to make achieving our New Year's resolutions a little easier? Of course there is!

The main reason why New Year's resolutions usually fall flat is because of high expectations. As the creative, quilty people we are, it's easy for us to take on more projects than we have time for, and we end up crowding our sewing rooms with beautiful but unfinished quilts! So, what is the resolution solution? It's simple: set realistic goals. Instead of attempting to tackle that colorful mountain of unfinished projects, choose the less time consuming ones. Or if you're an eager beginner who's new to quilting, don't overwhelm yourself with a complicated pattern, try something easy and fun!

Once you feel confident that you've found an achievable resolution, the next thing to consider is how meaningful it is. Sometimes New Year's resolutions are short lived because they don't bring any positive changes to our lives. Before you commit yourself to picking up a new hobby or making any kind of change in 2019, think about how it'll improve your life! For

example, if you think you drink a little too much coffee, cut back and see how much better you'll feel. If you feel like you spend too much time on your phone, reduce screen time and devote your attention to other things you enjoy!

As long as we keep these tips in mind, we'll all be ready to tackle and accomplish our New Year's resolutions. Now, it's time to relax, sip some hot cider, and look forward to all the joy and possibilities that 2019 has in store for us all.

materials

QUILT SIZE
86" x 104"

BLOCK SIZE
16" finished

QUILT TOP
1 package of 10" print squares
1 package of 10" background squares
2 yards background fabric
  - includes inner border

OUTER BORDER
1¾ yards

BINDING
¾ yard

BACKING
8 yards - horizontal seam(s)

SAMPLE QUILT
All Weather Friend by April Rosenthal
for Moda Fabrics

1 cut

From the background fabric, cut:

- (16) 2½" strips across the width of
  the fabric. Subcut 15 strips into 2½"
  x 16½" rectangles. Cut 1 rectangle
  from the remaining strip. Each strip
  will yield **2 rectangles** and a total of
  31 rectangles are needed. Set aside
  to use for sashing. Set aside the
  remainder of the fabric for the
  inner border.

From the outer border fabric, cut:

- (1) 2½" strip across the width of the
  fabric. Cut (12) 2½" squares from the
  strip. Set aside the squares to use as
  cornerstones when making sashing.

From the packages of 10" squares,
select **20 print** and **20 background
squares**.

Note: As you choose the prints, you
might want to keep in mind that most
of these pieces will be used for the
"thread" seen in the center of each
spool.

Cut each square in half vertically and
horizontally to make 5" squares. Trim (2)
5" print squares and (2) 5" background
squares to 4½". Keep all matching prints
together. You will have a **total of 40** of
each piece.

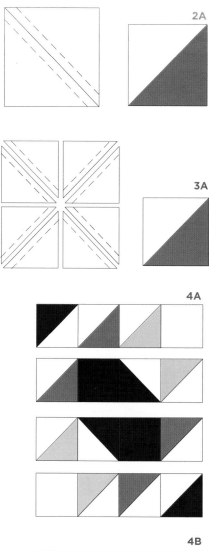

2 sew

On the reverse side of each of the 5" background squares, draw a line from corner to corner once on the diagonal. Layer a marked 5" background square with a 5" print square with right sides facing. Sew on both sides of the drawn line using a ¼" seam allowance. Cut on the drawn line and open to reveal 2 half-square triangle units. Press the seam allowance toward the darker fabric. Square each half-square triangle to 4½". Repeat for the remaining 5" squares. Again, keep all matching prints together and remember that these are the pieces that make up the thread. For the sake of clarity, let's group all of these pieces together and call them **Group 1. 2A**

3 layer and sew

From the packages of 10" squares, select **20 print squares** and **20 background squares**. Draw a line from corner to corner twice on the diagonal on the reverse side of each of the background squares. Place a marked background square atop a print square with right sides facing and sew on both sides of each of the drawn lines. Cut through the center of the sewn squares horizontally and vertically. Then cut on the drawn lines. Each set of sewn squares will yield 8 half-square triangle units for a **total of 160**. Square each half-square triangle to 4½". Keep all matching prints together. Let's group all of these together and call them **Group 2. 3A**

4 block construction

Pick up the following pieces before you begin to sew.

From Group 1:
4 matching half-square triangle units (thread and 2 corners)
2 matching 4½" squares
2 background 4½" squares

From Group 2:
4 matching half-square triangles of 1 print (top and bottom of spool)
4 matching half-square triangles of another print (hourglass)

We'll be making the block in rows. Each row is made up of **4 units** and you need **4 rows**. Lay out the block as shown. Be aware of the color placement. All the pieces making up the thread as well as the corners of the block are made using fabrics from **Group 1.** The hourglass portion as well as the spools come from **Group 2. 4A**

After you are satisfied that the block is laid out correctly, sew the units into rows. Then sew the rows together to complete the block. **Make 20. 4B**.

Block Size: 16" finished

5 arrange and sew

Lay out the blocks in rows. Each row is made up of **4 blocks** and **5 rows** are needed. Refer to the diagram on page 71 and notice how the blocks are oriented. As you sew the blocks

1 Layer a marked 5" background square with a 5" print square with right sides facing. Sew on both sides of the marked line using a ¼" seam allowance. Cut on the drawn line, open to reveal 2 half-square triangle units. Square each unit to 4½". Keep all matching prints together.

2 Place a marked 10" background square atop a 10" print square with right sides facing. Sew on both sides of each of the drawn lines. Cut through the center of the sewn squares horizontally and vertically. Then cut on the drawn lines. Open to reveal 8 half-square triangle units and square each to 4½". Keep all matching prints together.

3 Lay out the block as shown, being aware of color placement. Each block is made up of 4 rows and 4 rows are needed.

4 Sew the 4 rows together to complete each block. Make 20 blocks.

into rows, add a 2½" x 16½" background rectangle vertically between each block. Press the seam allowances toward the sashing strips.

Make horizontal sashing strips by sewing cornerstones and sashing rectangles together. Begin with a 2½" x 16½" sashing rectangle and add a cornerstone. Continue alternating the 2 pieces until you have a strip made up of **4 rectangles** and **3 cornerstones**. **Make 4.** Press the seam allowances toward the sashing rectangles. **5A**

Sew the rows together, adding a horizontal sashing strip between each.

6 inner border

Cut (9) 2½" strips across the width of the fabric. Sew the strips together end-to-end to make one long strip. Trim the borders from this strip.

Refer to Borders (pg. 102) in the Construction Basics to measure and cut the inner borders. The strips are approximately 88½" for the sides and approximately 74½" for the top and bottom.

7 outer border

Cut (9) 6½" strips across the width of the fabric. Sew the strips together end-to-end to make one long strip. Trim the borders from this strip.

Refer to Borders (pg. 102) in the Construction Basics to measure and cut the outer borders. The strips are approximately 92½" for the sides and approximately 86½" for the top and bottom.

8 quilt and bind

Layer the quilt with batting and backing and quilt. After the quilting is complete, square up the quilt and trim away all excess batting and backing. Add binding to complete the quilt. See Construction Basics (pg. 102) for binding instructions.

tranquil
triangles

When the days are frigid and the nights are long, you may feel tempted to follow the example of a big brown bear who hides away, keeping warm as the chill of winter passes him by. Of course, if you do, you'll miss so much!

Why not emulate a different sort of creature? One that braves the cold with a merry little tune on it's lips . . . erm . . . beak.

Every year, I watch in amazement as sweet little birds flock to my yard to pass the chilly hours in a cheerful flurry of chirps and feathers. How do they stay warm? Where do they sleep? Can they find enough food to fill their little tummies?

The truth is, birds are quite good at weathering cold temperatures. Their bodies are designed to stay warm in even the chilliest weather. If you've ever owned a down-filled coat, you've felt the incredible insulating power of feathers.

When it's cold outside, birds puff up their feathers to create air pockets around their little bodies. The air gets warm, and the feathers hold in that heat—just like a thick, cozy blanket. They tuck their tiny feet up into their feathers one at a time, and keep their noses buried deep in downy warmth. During the day, they soak up sunny rays and at night they snuggle in groups to share warmth.

For the tutorial and everything you need to make this quilt visit:
www.msqc.co/blockearlywinter18

72

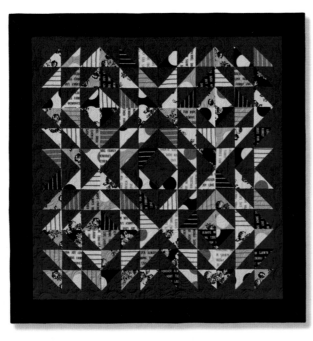

Even though Mother Nature has outfitted her little birds so carefully, a harsh winter can still take its toll. However, you can take a few simple steps to keep the birds in your neighborhood safe and happy all winter long.

Invest in a simple birdhouse. Make sure it's sturdy enough to keep bitter breezes from sneaking in. Add a nice layer of dried grass or wood shavings for extra coziness. Birds also love snuggling up in evergreens, hollow trees, and dense shrubs.

Fill your feeders with calorie-rich foods such as seeds, suet, nuts, and peanut butter. Don't just toss out a handful of nutritionless breadcrumbs! If you're hoping to see a variety of birds, set out a variety of quality foods. Each species of bird has its own favorites. You'll soon discover that some birds pick out all the sunflower seeds while others prefer the peanuts.

Be sure to provide water that is fresh and unfrozen. In a pinch, birds can get water from snow and ice, but it wastes a lot of energy. A heated bird bath can be a lifesaver during a hard freeze.

This year, take a few minutes to transform your yard into a safe haven for birds. Not only will the local birds be chipper and comfy, you'll have a ball watching them frolick. Studies show that caring for birds is actually more beneficial to humans that it is to birds! We can't help but feel more cheerful with a winged friend or two in our midst!

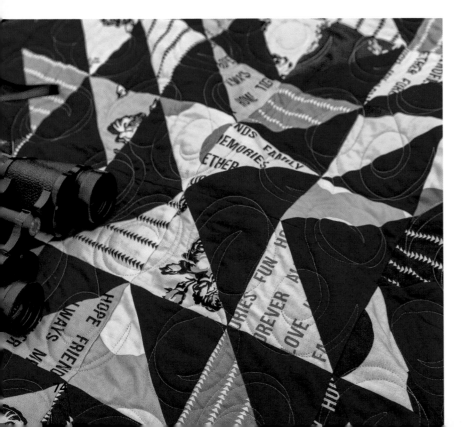

materials

QUILT SIZE
61" x 61" finished

BLOCK SIZE
12" finished

QUILT TOP
1 package 10" print squares
2 yards background fabric
  - includes inner border

OUTER BORDER
1 yard

BINDING
¾ yard

BACKING
4 yards - vertical seam(s)

SAMPLE QUILT
Urban Cottage by Urban Chiks
for Moda Fabrics

1 cut

From the background fabric, cut:

- (5) 10" strips across the width of the fabric - subcut 4 strips into 10" squares and cut (2) 10" squares from the 5th strip. You will have a **total of 18 squares.** Set aside the remainder of the strip for another project and use the rest of the yardage when cutting the inner border.

2 make half-square triangles

On the reverse side of each 10" background square, draw a line from corner to corner twice on the diagonal. Select 18 print squares from the package. Layer a background square with a print

2A

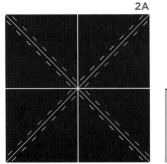

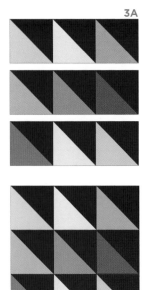

3A

square with right sides facing. Sew on both sides of the drawn lines using a ¼" seam allowance. Cut the sewn squares through the center horizontally and vertically, then on the drawn lines. Each sewn set of squares will yield 8 half-square triangle units, and you need a **total of 144. 2A**

3 block construction

Lay out 9 half-square triangle units in 3 rows of 3. Sew the rows together to complete 1 block. **Make 16. 3A**

Block Size: 12" finished.

4 arrange and sew

Lay out the blocks in rows. Each row is made up of **4 blocks** and **4 rows** are needed. Refer to the diagram on page 79 and notice the way each block is turned. After the blocks have been sewn into rows, press the seam allowances in the odd rows toward the right and the even rows toward the left to make the seams "nest."

5 inner border

Cut (6) 2½" strips across the width of the fabric. Sew the strips together end-to-end to make one long strip. Trim the borders from this strip.

Refer to Borders (pg. 102) in the Construction Basics to measure and cut the inner borders. The strips are approximately 48½" for the sides and approximately 52½" for the top and bottom.

6 outer border

Cut (6) 5" strips across the width of the fabric. Sew the strips together end-to-end to make one long strip. Trim the borders from this strip.

Refer to Borders (pg. 102) in the Construction Basics to measure and cut the outer borders. The strips are approximately 52½" for the sides and approximately 61½" for the top and bottom.

1 On the reverse side of each background square, draw a line from corner to corner twice on the diagonal. Layer a marked background square with a print square with right sides facing. Sew on either side of the drawn lines using a ¼" seam allowance. Cut the sewn squares in half horizontally and vertically, then cut on the drawn lines. Open, press and square each unit to 4½".

2 Sew 3 half-square triangle units together as shown to make a row. Make 3 rows.

3 Sew the 3 rows together to complete one block.

7 quilt and bind

Layer the quilt with batting and backing and quilt. After the quilting is complete, square up the quilt and trim away all excess batting and backing. Add binding to complete the quilt. See Construction Basics (pg. 102) for binding instructions.

twist and *shout*

It's 11:59 pm on December 31st. The countdown begins. Ten. Nine. Eight. Seven. Six. Five. Four. Three. Two. One. Happy New Year!

What will you be doing as 2018 becomes 2019? Well, it all depends on where you live. Every culture has its own traditions; perhaps you'll add one or two to your own celebration this year. Here are a few suggestions:

In Spain, you can secure 12 months of good luck by eating grapes at midnight. It sounds easy, but it's not! At the stroke of midnight, pop in the first grape and start chewing like crazy, because you've got to add another grape with each chime of the clock. That's 12 grapes in 12 seconds! If you succeed, you're sure to have a lovely 12 months. (Careful! You don't want to choke to death in those first few moments of the new year!)

In Brazil, folks wear lucky undies on New Year's Eve: Yellow if they're hoping for money; red if they're looking for love.

For the tutorial and everything you need to make this quilt visit:
www.msqc.co/blockearlywinter18

80

Filipinos attract prosperity for the new year by celebrating with circles—the symbol of wealth. Round fruits on the table, pockets full of jangling coins, and even polkadot outfits!

And if you are a single lady hoping for wedding bells in the new year, Belarus has the answer! On New Year's Eve, single ladies sit in a circle. A pile of corn is placed in front of each, and then a rooster is let loose. The gal who's pile of corn attracts the rooster first is sure to be wed in the coming year!

Of course, if travel is on your wishlist for the new year, you don't have to depend on a rooster to grant your heart's desire; just grab your luggage! According to Colombian custom, simply march around the block with your empty suitcases, and it's "bon voyage!" for you!

And finally, if you're up for a delicious challenge, I suggest the Estonian tradition of eating seven meals on New Year's Day. If you succeed, not only will you have proven that you have the strength of seven men (or ladies, of course), but you can also expect an abundance of good eats in the new year! Woohoo!

However you choose to celebrate, I hope you have a wonderful new year filled with the happiest wishes of your heart!

materials

QUILT SIZE
70" x 70"

BLOCK SIZE
12" finished

QUILT TOP
1 roll of 2½" print strips
2¼ yards background fabric
  - includes inner border

OUTER BORDER
1 yard

BINDING
¾ yard

BACKING
4½ yards - vertical seam(s)
or 2¼ yards 90" wide

SAMPLE QUILT
Dance of the Dragonfly by Kanvas
Studios for Benartex

1 cut

From the background fabric, cut:

- (8) 4½" strips across the width of fabric – subcut strips into 4½" squares. Each strip will yield 8 squares and a **total of 64 squares** are needed.

- (14) 2½" strips across the width of fabric – subcut 8 strips into 2½" x 12½" rectangles. Each strip will yield 3 rectangles and a **total of 24 rectangles** are needed. Set the remaining 6 strips aside for the inner border.

Set aside 24 of the 2½" strips from your roll for use in making the strip sets.

From the remaining strips, cut:

- (4) 2½" x 6½" rectangles from each strip. A **total of 64 rectangles** are needed.

Select 9 of these 2½" strips and cut (1) 2½" square from each. A **total of 9 squares** are needed.

From the outer border fabric, cut:

- (5) 6½" strips across the width of the fabric.

2A

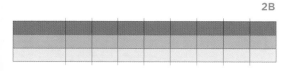

2B

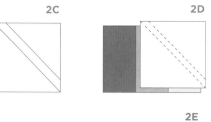

2C   2D

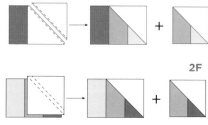

2E

2F

2G

2H   2I

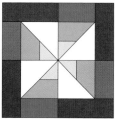

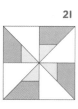

3A

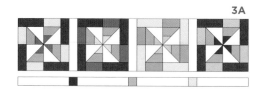

2 make pinwheel blocks

Using the (24) 2½" strips you set aside, sew them together in sets of 3 along the length to create a strip set. Press seam allowances toward one side. **2A**

Cut each strip set into (8) 4½" x 6½" identical rectangle strip units. Cut a **total of 64 rectangle strip units. 2B**

On the wrong side of each of the 4½" background squares, draw a line diagonally from corner to corner. Draw another line ½" away from this line. **2C**

Place a background square right sides together, matching the right edge of the square to the right edge of a rectangle strip unit, with the drawn lines going from the top left of the square to the bottom right. Stitch diagonally across the square along both drawn lines. **2D**

Cut between the seams at the halfway point. **2E**

Trim the smaller pieced half-square triangle unit to 3½" and set it aside to make the border pinwheel blocks.

Make 4 identical units. With the remaining 4 rectangle strip units cut from the same strip set, rotate them 180° before stitching the square to the unit. **2F**

Repeat to make 16 sets of 4 identical units for a **total of 64 units.**

Select a set of (4) 2½" x 6½" rectangles and a set of 4 identical pieced units. Sew the rectangles along the tops of the pieced units. Press the seam allowances toward the rectangles. **2G**

Arrange the 4 identical units into a pinwheel and sew together to make the block. **2H**

Repeat to make a **total of 16 pinwheel blocks.**

Block size: 12" finished

Using the smaller pieced half-square triangles you set aside earlier, arrange the 4 identical small pieced half-square triangle units into a pinwheel and sew together to make the small pinwheel blocks for the border. **2I**

3 arrange and sew

Lay out the large blocks in **4 rows** made up of **4 blocks** separated by (3) 2½" x 12½" sashing strips. Between the rows of blocks, there are 3 rows of sashing made up of (4) 2½" x 12½" sashing strips and (3) 2½" cornerstone squares. Sew the rows together to complete the center of the quilt. **3A**

4 inner border

Sew the 6 strips together end-to-end to make 1 long strip. Trim the borders from this strip.

Refer to Borders (pg. 102) in the Construction Basics to measure and cut the inner borders. The strips are approximately 54½" for the sides and approximately 58½" for the top and bottom.

5 outer border

Sew 4 of the small pinwheels you made in section 2 together to form a row. **5A**

Repeat to make a **total of 4 rows.**

Sew 3 of the border strips together end-to-end to make one long strip. Cut this long strip in half. Sew (1) 6½" border strip to the right edge of each row of small pinwheel blocks. Press toward the border fabric. **5B**

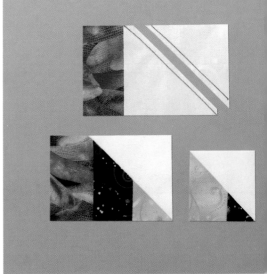

1 Sew (3) 2½" strips together along the length to create a strip set. Press all the seam allowances in the same direction.

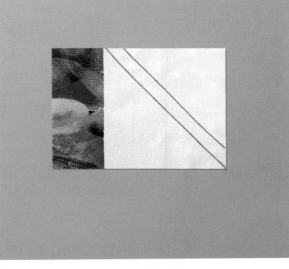

2 Cut each strip set into (8) 4½" x 6½" rectangles. Draw a line from corner to corner on the reverse side of a 4½" background square and another line ½" from the first. Place the marked square atop the rectangle and sew on both lines.

3 Cut between the sewn seams. Trim the smaller pieced half-square triangle to 3½" and set aside to use in the border.

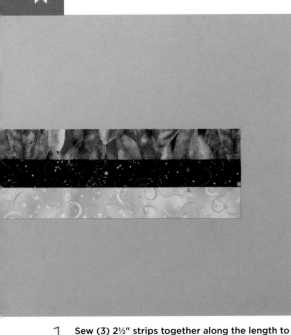

4 Flip a strip set so the dark strip is on the opposite end as before. Repeat the previous instructions and sew a marked 4½" background square atop the rectangle. Cut between the sewn seams and trim the smaller half-square triangle to 3½".

86

5 Select 4 matching 2½" x 6½" rectangles and a set of 4 matching pieced units. Sew a rectangle to each pieced unit. Make 4.

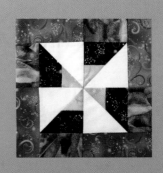

6 Sew the 4 matching units into a pinwheel as shown. Sew 4 small matching small half-square triangles together into a pinwheel as well and set them aside to use in the border.

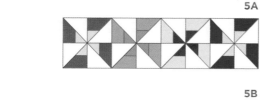

5A

5B

—Start measuring from this end

5C

Note: 2 of these borders will be longer than the other 2. The longer borders are for the top and bottom of the quilt.

Measure the height of your quilt in 3 places as explained in Borders (pg. 102) in the Construction Basics.

Using the measurement you determined for the height of your quilt, cut the 2 shorter borders to this length. Be sure to start measuring from the side with the pinwheels and cut only the border strip fabric. **5C**

This pair of borders will be approximately 58½" in length.

Sew these borders to the sides of the quilt. Press toward the quilt center.

Measure the width of your quilt in 3 places as explained in Borders (pg. 102) in the Construction Basics.

Using the measurement you determined for the width of your quilt, cut the 2 remaining borders in the same manner as before. Sew these borders to the top and bottom of the quilt. Press toward the quilt center.

This pair of borders will be approximately 70½" in length.

6 quilt and bind

Layer the quilt with batting and backing and quilt. After the quilting is complete, square up the quilt and trim away all excess batting and backing. Add binding to complete the quilt. See the Construction Basics (pg. 102) for binding instructions.

yo-yo quilts

Yo-yos are cute, gathered, circles of fabric that are used in a variety of sewing projects—from whimsical coverlets and wall hangings to tablecloths, toys, pillows, fashion accessories, and more! Also known as Suffolk puffs, these fun little fabric adornments have become a favorite again in the quilting world.

From the 1920s to the 1940s, yo-yos were fashionable in the United States, but their history may date back as early as the 1600s in England. Suffolk puffs were created by hardworking folks who wanted to use up every scrap of fabric and also create something decorative. Some were then stuffed with wool and stitched together into ingenious quilts that were both beautiful and functional.

When yo-yos came to the U.S., they were often stitched up in cheerful prints that were popular at the time. They are still associated with reproduction prints and are often created from those fabrics, but they can be made from any fabric that quilters have on hand. They're great for stitching on the go and don't require any quilting to finish. My grandmother wasn't a quilter, but she loved making yo-yos and she made her grandchildren toys and dolls with them.

How are yo-yos made? Using either a template or a circular piece of cardboard, cut out a circle of fabric. Depending on how large you would like your yo-yo to be, plan on double the circumference as it will be gathered in on itself. Take a needle and thread, make a knot at the end, and sew a running stitch ¼" in all around the edge. If you would like to add stuffing, now is the time. Put a small amount inside the puff and cinch the fabric around it until it's fully enclosed. Turn the raw edges under. Then, stitch through to the other side and knot the thread to finish. And that's all there is to it! There are also notions out there that make creating yo-yos even easier.

Try adding yo-yos to a tote bag for extra appeal, or create a charming pillow to accent your decor. If you're feeling ambitious, really go for it and make a gorgeous coverlet for your bed! No matter how you use them, it's bound to be a blast. Give yo-yos a try and you may find yourself coming back to these cuties again and again!

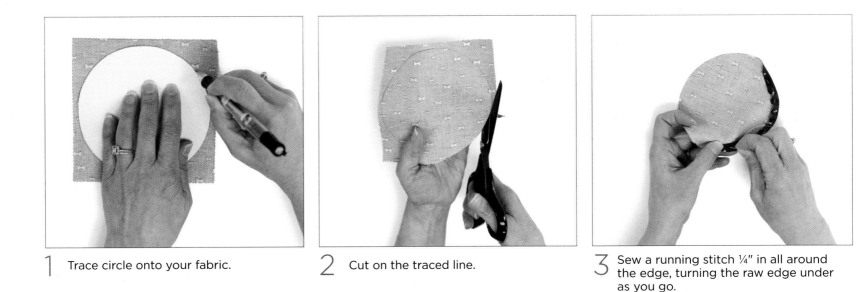

1   Trace circle onto your fabric.

2   Cut on the traced line.

3   Sew a running stitch ¼" in all around the edge, turning the raw edge under as you go.

4   When you get to back to the beginning of your stitches, pull the thread gently. This will gather your stitches together closing the circle and creating your yo-yo.

5   Stitch through to the other side and knot the thread to finish your yo-yo.

6   You're done!

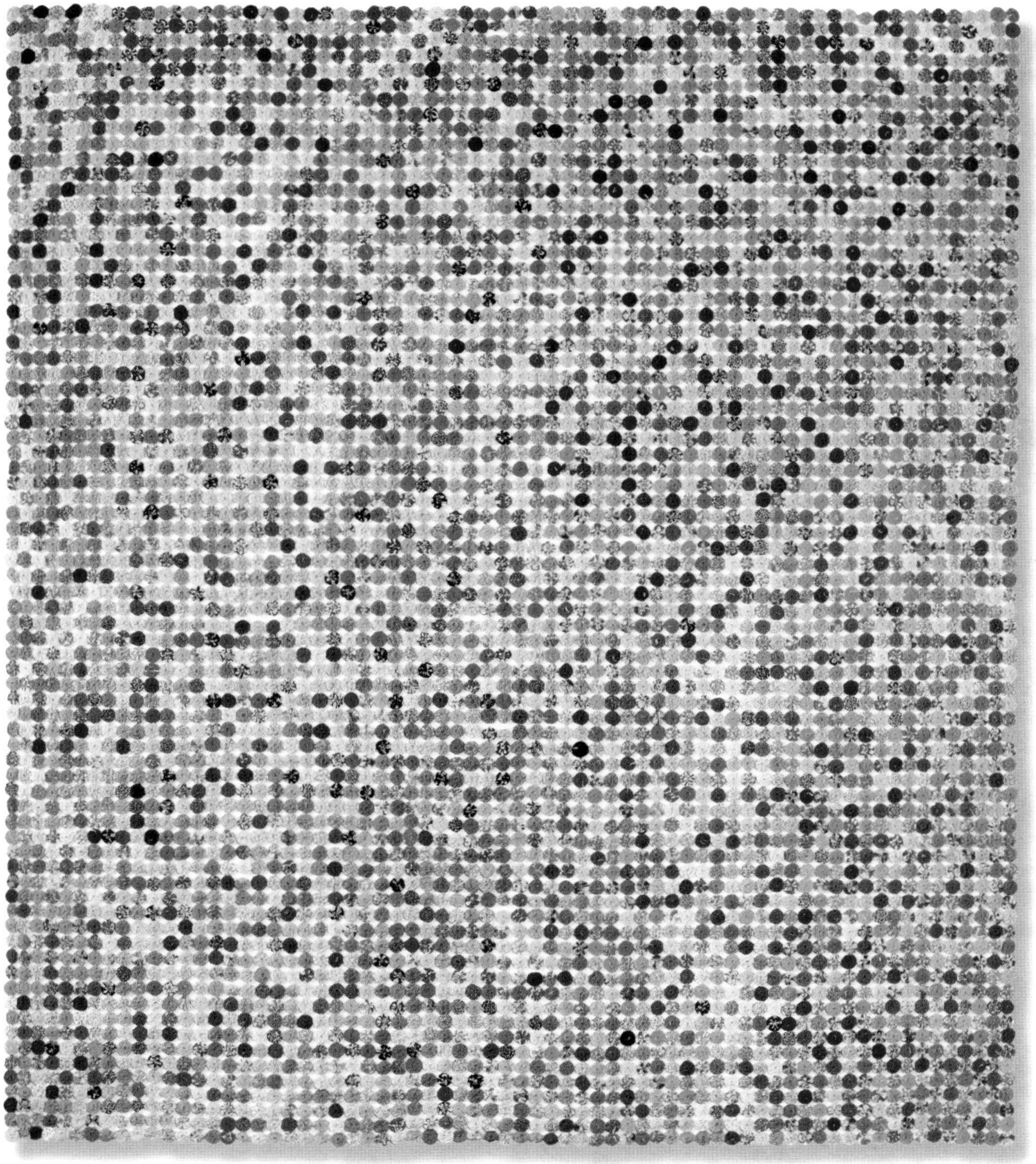

baskets of blooms

QUILT SIZE
71" x 85"

BLOCK SIZE
14" finished

QUILT TOP
1 roll of 2½" strips
3½ yards background fabric
  - includes inner border
1¼ yards complementary fabric

OUTER BORDER
1½ yards

BINDING
¾ yard

BACKING
5¼ yards - vertical seam(s)

SAMPLE QUILT
Farm Girl Vintage by Lori Holt of
Bee in my Bonnet for Riley Blake
Designs

QUILTING PATTERN
Simply Roses

ONLINE TUTORIALS
msqc.co/blockearlywinter18

PATTERN
pg. 6

candy twist

QUILT SIZE
70" x 79½"

BLOCK SIZE
9½" finished

QUILT TOP
2 packages of 5" print squares
1 package of 5" background squares
4 yards background fabric
  - includes innermost and
    outermost borders

PIECED BORDER
¼ yard complementary fabric

BINDING
¾ yard

BACKING
5 yards - vertical seam(s)

SAMPLE QUILT
Adeline by Kathy Hall for
Andover Fabrics

QUILTING PATTERN
Sticky Buns

ONLINE TUTORIALS
msqc.co/blockearlywinter18

PATTERN
pg. 14

little stitches

WALL HANGING SIZE
36" x 49½" finished

BLOCK SIZE
4½" finished

WALL HANGING TOP
1 package 5" print squares
½ yard background fabric
¼ yard complementary fabric

BORDER
¾ yard

BINDING
½ yard

BACKING
1¾ yards

OTHER MATERIALS
½ yard lightweight fusible web

SAMPLE QUILT
Scribbles Single Scoops by
Andover Fabrics

QUILTING PATTERN
A Notion to Sew

ONLINE TUTORIALS
msqc.co/blockearlywinter18

PATTERN
pg. 24

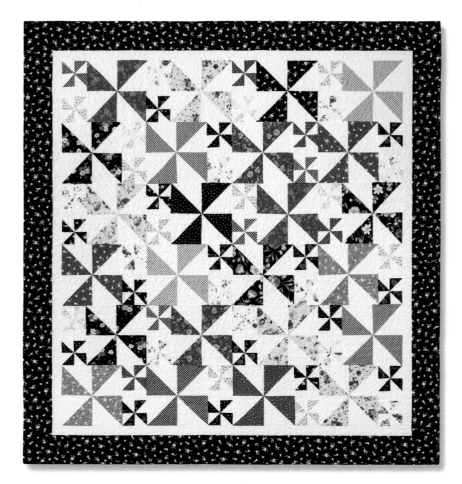

pinwheel picnic

QUILT SIZE
83" X 87"

BLOCK SIZE
17" x 12" finished

QUILT TOP
1 package 10" print squares
1 package 10" background squares
1 yard of background fabric
   - includes inner border

OUTER BORDER
1½ yards

BINDING
¾ yard

BACKING
8 yards - vertical seam(s)
   or 2¾ yards 108" wide

SAMPLE QUILT
Afternoon Picnic by Nancy Zieman
Productions for Penny Rose Fabrics

QUILTING PATTERN
Cotton Candy

ONLINE TUTORIALS
msqc.co/blockearlywinter18

PATTERN
pg. 32

scallop city

QUILT SIZE
56" x 66"

BLOCK SIZE
6" x 4" finished

QUILT TOP
1 roll of 2½" print strips
1¼ yards background fabric
 - includes inner border

OUTER BORDER
1 yard

BINDING
¾ yard

BACKING
3½ yards - horizontal seam(s)

SAMPLE QUILT
Fruitful Pleasures by Lila Tueller
for Riley Blake Designs

QUILTING PATTERN
Champagne Bubbles

ONLINE TUTORIALS
msqc.co/blockearlywinter18

PATTERN
pg. 40

star patch

QUILT SIZE
76" x 88"

BLOCK SIZE
8" finished

QUILT TOP
1 roll of 2½" print strips
1½ yards complementary fabric
4½ yards background fabric

BINDING
¾ yard

BACKING
7 yards - horizontal seam(s)

SAMPLE QUILT
Tickled Pink by Janet Rae Nesbit
of One Sister Designs for Henry Glass
Fabrics

QUILTING PATTERN
Stars and Loops

ONLINE TUTORIALS
msqc.co/blockearlywinter18

PATTERN
pg. 48

sundance

QUILT SIZE
37" x 43"

BLOCK SIZE
6" finished

QUILT TOP
1 package of 5" print squares
1 package of 5" background squares

INNER BORDER
¼ yard

OUTER BORDER
¾ yard

BINDING
½ yard

BACKING
2½ yards - horizontal seam(s)

OTHER
1 Moda Cupcake Mix Recipe
Foundation Paper Pattern Pad #4

SAMPLE QUILT
Home Again by Jill Finley of Jillily
Studios for Penny Rose Fabrics

QUILTING PATTERN
Daisy Days

ONLINE TUTORIALS
msqc.co/blockearlywinter18

PATTERN
pg. 56

time to sew

QUILT SIZE
86" x 104"

BLOCK SIZE
16" finished

QUILT TOP
1 package of 10" print squares
1 package of 10" background squares
2 yards background fabric
  - includes inner border

OUTER BORDER
1¾ yards

BINDING
¾ yard

BACKING
8 yards - horizontal seam(s)

SAMPLE QUILT
All Weather Friend by April Rosenthal for Moda Fabrics

QUILTING PATTERN
Spools of Thread

ONLINE TUTORIALS
msqc.co/blockearlywinter18

PATTERN
pg. 64

tranquil triangles

QUILT SIZE
61" x 61" finished

BLOCK SIZE
12" finished

QUILT TOP
1 package 10" print squares
2 yards background fabric
  - includes inner border

OUTER BORDER
1 yard

BINDING
¾ yard

BACKING
4 yards - vertical seam(s)

SAMPLE QUILT
Urban Cottage by Urban Chiks
for Moda Fabrics

QUILTING PATTERN
Wind Swirls

ONLINE TUTORIALS
msqc.co/blockearlywinter18

PATTERN
pg. 72

twist and shout

QUILT SIZE
70" x 70"

BLOCK SIZE
12" finished

QUILT TOP
1 roll of 2½" print strips
2¼ yards background fabric
  - includes inner border

OUTER BORDER
1 yard

BINDING
¾ yard

BACKING
4½ yards - vertical seam(s)
or 2¼ yards 90" wide

SAMPLE QUILT
Dance of the Dragonfly by Kanvas
Studios for Benartex

QUILTING PATTERN
Dragonflies

ONLINE TUTORIALS
msqc.co/blockearlywinter18

PATTERN
pg. 80

construction basics

general quilting

- All seams are ¼" inch unless directions specify differently.
- Cutting instructions are given at the point when cutting is required.
- Precuts are not prewashed; therefore do not prewash other fabrics in the project.
- All strips are cut width of fabric.
- Remove all selvages.

press seams

- Use a steam iron on the cotton setting.
- Press the seam just as it was sewn right sides together. This "sets" the seam.
- With dark fabric on top, lift the dark fabric and press back.
- The seam allowance is pressed toward the dark side. Some patterns may direct otherwise for certain situations.
- Follow pressing arrows in the diagrams when indicated.
- Press toward borders. Pieced borders may demand otherwise.
- Press diagonal seams open on binding to reduce bulk.

borders

- Always measure the quilt top 3 times before cutting borders.
- Start measuring about 4" in from each side and through the center vertically.
- Take the average of those 3 measurements.
- Cut 2 border strips to that size. Piece strips together if needed.
- Attach one to either side of the quilt.

- Position the border fabric on top as you sew. The feed dogs can act like rufflers. Having the border on top will prevent waviness and keep the quilt straight.
- Repeat this process for the top and bottom borders, measuring the width 3 times.
- Include the newly attached side borders in your measurements.
- Press toward the borders.

binding

find a video tutorial at: www.msqc.co/006

- Use 2½" strips for binding.
- Sew strips end-to-end into one long strip with diagonal seams, aka the plus sign method (next). Press seams open.
- Fold in half lengthwise wrong sides together and press.
- The entire length should equal the outside dimension of the quilt plus 15" - 20."

plus sign method

- Lay one strip across the other as if to make a plus sign right sides together.
- Sew from top inside to bottom outside corners crossing the intersections of fabric as you sew. Trim excess to ¼" seam allowance.
- Press seam open.

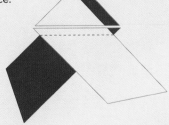

find a video tutorial at: www.msqc.co/001

attach binding

- Match raw edges of folded binding to the quilt top edge.
- Leave a 10" tail at the beginning.
- Use a ¼" seam allowance.
- Start in the middle of a long straight side.

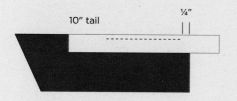

10" tail   ¼"

miter corners

- Stop sewing ¼" before the corner.
- Move the quilt out from under the presser foot.
- Clip the threads.
- Flip the binding up at a 90° angle to the edge just sewn.
- Fold the binding down along the next side to be sewn, aligning raw edges.
- The fold will lie along the edge just completed.
- Begin sewing on the fold.

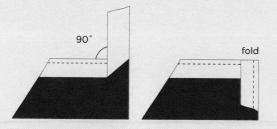

90°   fold

close binding

MSQC recommends The Binding Tool from TQM Products to finish binding perfectly every time.

- Stop sewing when you have 12" left to reach the start.
- Where the binding tails come together, trim excess leaving only 2½" of overlap.
- It helps to pin or clip the quilt together at the two points where the binding starts and stops. This takes the pressure off of the binding tails while you work.
- Use the plus sign method to sew the two binding ends together, except this time when making the plus sign, match the edges. Using a pencil, mark your sewing line because you won't be able to see where the corners intersect. Sew across.

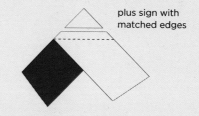

plus sign with matched edges

- Trim off excess; press seam open.
- Fold in half wrong sides together, and align all raw edges to the quilt top.
- Sew this last binding section to the quilt. Press.
- Turn the folded edge of the binding around to the back of the quilt and tack into place with an invisible stitch or machine stitch if you wish.